FUN
OF THE
FAIR

MELANiE McNEiCE

David and Charles

www.stitchcraftcreate.co.uk

CONTENTS

INTRODUCTION

Welcome to a world of excitement and adventure as our travelling show rolls into town. Amidst the beauty of the bunting, the sweet cotton candy, the prize-winning games and the pin-wheeling fireworks, best of all are the animals. From carousel ponies to parading elephants, from mischievous monkeys to fish-juggling seals, and an awesome lion, too, my circus creatures are free to be loved, played with and cuddled by all!

The patterns are suitable for all skill levels, and they are explained with step-by-step instructions, illustrated with beautiful colour photographs and diagrams. Actual-size templates are provided so you can get started straight away, and useful stitching techniques are also included. However, should you need a little more help, please visit my website and look through the fabulous tutorials section where there is even more advice to help you on your toy-making journey.

This book has truly been a joy to make – I was so excited to have the opportunity to revisit some of my all-time favourite animals and make them into new toy creations. I love each and every one, and I hope that they bring just as much delight to you and yours as they have to me.

MELLY

www.mellyandme.com

SAFETY NOTE: If making these toys for a small child, omit the buttons for the eyes and joining of the legs as they are a potential choking hazard; alternatives are provided in the steps.

PONY RIDES

When I was a little girl, my favourite part of any visit to the fair was always the pony rides. In my imaginary world, I had my very own pony. We were the best of friends and rode together all day long with the wind in our hair! Now I have designed this little carousel horse with her candy-coloured mane for your children to enjoy.

YOU WILL NEED

Note: Buttons should be omitted if making this toy for a very small child. Use a 100% cotton patchwork fabric with a width of 106cm–114cm (42in–44in).

★ 25cm (10in) x the full fabric width of the main fabric (body, legs)

★ 15cm (6in) x the full fabric width of the contrasting fabric (hooves, ears)

★ 5cm x 10cm (2in x 4in) lightweight fusible fleece

★ Two skeins of perle 5 variegated thread for mane/tail

★ Four 2.5cm (1in) buttons for button jointing

★ Six-strand embroidery thread (floss) in colour to match button-jointing buttons

★ Two small black buttons for eyes and black thread

★ Dollmaker's needle: 12.5cm (5in) or longer

★ Good-quality polyester thread

★ Good-quality polyester toy filling

FINISHED SIZE: 25cm (10in) tall x 23cm (9in) long

CUTTING YOUR FABRICS

Note: Trace the Pony Rides (orange) templates (see Templates) onto tracing paper or template plastic, transferring all of the markings, and cut them out around the traced lines. When using these templates to trace the pattern pieces onto your fabric, do ensure that the marked grain line on the template matches the fabric grain line.

FROM YOUR MAIN FABRIC:

Cut one piece of fabric measuring 25cm (10in) high x 46cm (18in) wide for the legs.

Fold remaining fabric in half with right sides together. Trace the body template once onto the wrong side of the folded fabric, transferring all markings. **Do not** cut out.

FROM YOUR CONTRASTING FABRIC:

Cut two strips measuring 7cm (2¾in) high x 46cm (18in) wide for the hooves.

Cut one piece measuring 10cm x 10cm (4in x 4in) for the ears.

Trace the hoof base template four times onto the remaining fabric and cut out along the traced lines.

PREPARING TO START

1. Interface one half of the 10cm (4in) contrasting fabric square with the lightweight fusible fleece.

2. Tail and mane: Take the perle 5 variegated thread and cut into 30 lengths, each measuring approx 1m (40in) long, placing them together in a neat, even bundle. Measuring 12.5cm (5in) from the end, wrap a very small piece of adhesive tape around the bundle to enclose the threads. Measure another 12.5cm (5in) along the length and, again, tape the threads together. Continue in this way to the end of the thread bundle to divide it into eight equal sections, ending with a piece of tape. Cut through the threads after each piece of tape to give you eight thread bundles, one for the tail and seven for the mane (see Fig. 1).

3. Set your sewing machine to a small stitch length of approx 1.5 for stitching the toy and use a good-quality polyester thread for strong seams (if cotton thread is used, your seams could break during stuffing).

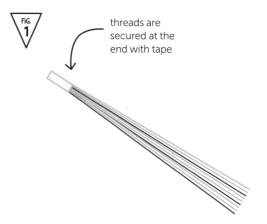

threads are secured at the end with tape

MAKING THE PONY

Note: A 6mm (¼in) seam allowance is included in all pattern pieces unless advised otherwise. Read through all instructions before beginning to avoid any surprises.

1. Take the main fabric piece with the pony body traced onto it, and machine stitch around the traced line leaving three gaps open as indicated by the broken lines on the template.

2. Cut out the pony body 6mm (¼in) outside the sewn/traced lines. **Do not** turn right side out.

3. Take one of the thread bundles and guide the taped end through the tummy gap in the pony body, to push it up through the tail gap so that the taped end is poking out;. Now stitch along the tail gap to secure the tail thread bundle in place (Fig. 2), and cut off the taped end.

4. Take your remaining seven thread bundles, ready to sew these into position along the gap on the top of the head to make the mane. Starting at the front (fringe region), position the thread bundles evenly along the gap so that the taped sections are poking out and the loose threads are sitting neatly inside the body. Clip or tack (baste) the thread bundles in place, then sew the gap closed along the traced line to secure the mane evenly in your stitching (Fig. 3). Cut off the taped ends.

5. Turn the body right side out through the turning gap in the tummy, and stuff firmly with toy filling. Ladder stitch the opening closed (see Stitching Techniques), adding a little more filling as you go to avoid a dimple.

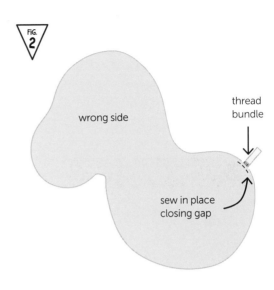

FIG. 2

wrong side

thread bundle

sew in place closing gap

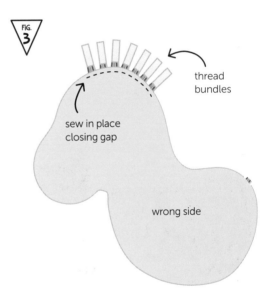

FIG. 3

thread bundles

sew in place closing gap

wrong side

TIP: IT MAY BE EASIER TO CLIP THE HAIR BUNDLES IN PLACE RATHER THAN PINNING OR TACKING (BASTING) THEM. IF YOU DON'T HAVE ANY SEWING CLIPS, SIMPLE METAL HAIR CLIPS WILL WORK, TOO.

6. Take the remaining main fabric (leg) piece and the two strips of contrasting (hoof) fabric each measuring 46cm (18in) long. Sew one of the contrasting (hoof) strips to each 46cm (18in) edge of the main fabric (Fig. 4). Press the seams well to the hoof fabric side.

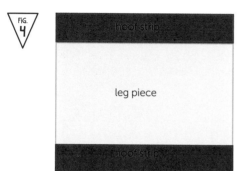

7. Fold the joined panel in half, right sides together, so that the two hoof fabric strips are sitting neatly and evenly on top of each other. Take the leg template and trace around it four times onto the panel making sure to align the straight (broken line) edge with the raw edge of the hoof fabric, leaving a 1.3cm (½in) space between each traced leg to allow for cutting out after stitching (see step 8).

8. Machine stitch the legs together along the traced lines, leaving the straight (broken line) edge unstitched. Cut out each leg approx 6mm (¼in) outside the sewn lines. **Do not** turn right side out.

9. Take one of the hoof base pieces and ease this into place, right sides facing, along the bottom raw edge of one of the legs. Tack (baste) well, then machine stitch in place. To ensure there is no puckering, it will help after each small section is sewn to stop stitching with the needle down, and to rotate and smooth the leg fabric underneath before continuing. Complete all four legs.

10. To turn the legs right side out, cut the small turning slit as marked on the template on **one side only** of each leg (single fabric thickness). Stuff each leg firmly with toy filling, then ladder stitch the opening closed (because the turning gaps will be hidden against the body of the pony, there is no need to worry about perfect stitching).

11. Now button joint the front legs to the front of the pony's body, referring to Fig. 5. Thread the dollmaker's needle with a long length of six-strand embroidery thread (floss). Tie a double knot in the end of your length of thread and trim close to the knot. Start by threading the needle through one side of the pony's body at the desired leg location (refer to photograph as a positioning guide), taking it right through the body and out the other side at exactly the same level. Thread the needle through one of the legs, then through one

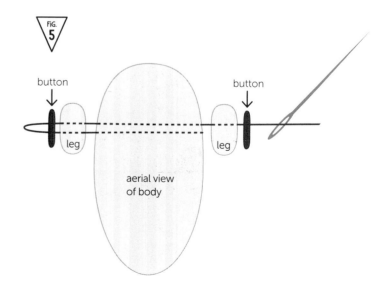

of the buttons, then go back through all of the layers again (button, leg, body) to come back out close to your start point. Here, thread the needle through the remaining leg and button (as shown in Fig. 5) and return again through the body to the other side. Continue in the same way, taking the needle through all the layers a few times, pulling the threads taut after each pass through. Tie off your thread and sink the knot into the leg (see Stitching Techniques).

12. Repeat the button joining process to attach the back legs to the back of the body. Attach the back legs slightly higher than the front legs.

13. Take your ear fabric square and fold it in half with right sides together, so that one side is interfaced and one side is not. Trace around the ear template twice onto the interfaced side. Machine stitch along the traced lines, leaving the turning gap open as indicated by the broken line on the template. Snip the corners, turn through to the right side and press.

14. Using a strong polyester thread, ladder stitch the base of the ears onto the pony's head working first along the front edge, then along the back edge for added strength.

TIP: IF YOU ARE MAKING THIS TOY FOR A SMALL CHILD, JOIN THE LEGS AS IN STEP 11 BUT WITHOUT THE BUTTONS. FOR THE EYES, USE SMALL CIRCLES OF BLACK WOOL FELT OR CREATE WITH SATIN STITCH (SEE STITCHING TECHNIQUES).

15. Using black thread, sew the button eyes into place on the pony's face, referring to the finished toy photograph for positioning. Sew into place following the same method as for button jointing the legs (see step 11), pulling the thread to indent the eyes ever so slightly if desired. (Remember: if making this toy for a very small child, you should omit the button eyes.)

16. To finish the pony, trim the mane as you prefer: I cut the front section a little shorter to make a fringe, then trimmed the remainder until I was pleased with the overall effect.

ELEPHANT PARADE

ONE GREY ELEPHANT BALANCING,
STEP BY STEP ON A PIECE OF STRING,
HE THOUGHT IT WAS SUCH A WONDERFUL STUNT,
THAT HE CALLED FOR ANOTHER ELEPHANT.

I fondly remember my children singing this tune when they were little and I will admit that I found myself singing it constantly as I created this cute elephant family for you to make for yours.

YOU WILL NEED

Note: Buttons should be omitted if making this toy for a very small child. Use a 100% cotton patchwork fabric with a width of 106cm–114cm (42in–44in).

(FOR ONE ELEPHANT)

★ 21cm (8in) x the full fabric width of the main body fabric (body, inner legs)

★ 20cm x 25cm (8in x 10in) contrasting fabric (ear)

★ 20cm x 12.5cm (8in x 5in) lightweight fusible fleece

★ 10cm (4in) of matching cord for tail

★ 100% wool felt for eyes: one piece white 5cm x 7.5cm (2in x 3in) and one piece blue 2.5cm x 5cm (1in x 2in)

★ 7.5cm x 7.5cm (3in x 3in) fusible web

★ Two small black buttons for pupils and black thread

★ Good-quality polyester thread

★ Good-quality polyester toy filling

FINISHED SIZES: Mummy/Daddy 15cm (6in) tall x 20cm (8in) long; Baby 12.5cm (5in) tall x 16.5cm (6½in) long

CUTTING YOUR FABRICS

Note: Trace the Elephant Parade (green) templates (see Templates) onto tracing paper or template plastic, transferring all of the markings, and cut them out around the traced lines. When using these templates to trace the pattern pieces onto your fabric, do ensure that the marked grain line on the template matches the fabric grain line.

FROM YOUR MAIN FABRIC:

Fold the fabric in half with right sides together. Trace the body and inner leg templates once onto the wrong side of the folded fabric, transferring all markings. Cut out along the traced lines to give you two mirror-image pieces of each.

FROM YOUR CONTRASTING FABRIC:

Fold the fabric in half with right sides together and trace the ear template twice onto the wrong side of the folded fabric. Cut out along the traced lines to give you four ear pieces.

FROM LIGHTWEIGHT FUSIBLE FLEECE:

Trace the ear template twice onto the fleece, flipping the template for your second trace. Cut out along the traced lines.

PREPARING TO START

1. Interface two of the fabric ear pieces with the matching fusible fleece pieces.

2. Trace the inner and outer eyes twice each onto the paper side of the fusible web and rough cut out. Fuse the inner eyes to the blue felt and the outer eyes to the white felt, and cut out along the traced lines.

3. Set your sewing machine to a small stitch length of approx 1.5 for stitching the toy and use a good-quality polyester thread for strong seams (if cotton thread is used, your seams could break during stuffing).

MAKING THE ELEPHANT

Note: A 6mm (¼in) seam allowance is included in all pattern pieces unless advised otherwise. Read through all instructions before beginning to avoid surprises.

1. First attach the eyes to the body pieces. Peel off the backing paper from the white outer eye pieces and fuse in place on the body pieces as marked on the template. Machine appliqué into position using white thread. Repeat to fix the blue inner eye pieces in position, making sure to change to a matching thread colour. Hand sew a small black button in place for the pupil (see photograph for positioning guide).

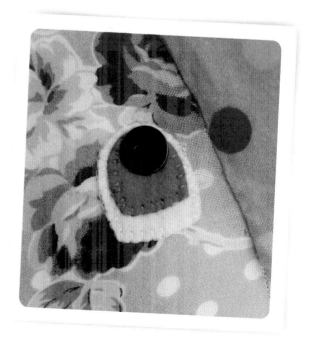

2. Take one of the body pieces and your length of matching cord. Secure the cord ends with a little adhesive tape to avoid fraying. Position the cord onto the body piece, right sides together, so that one raw end meets the tail position marked on the template (Fig. 1). Machine tack (baste) the cord tail into place.

3. Pair up the ear pieces, one with fleece with one without fleece, and place together with right sides facing. Pin, then machine sew each pair together, leaving the inner edges open for turning as indicated by the broken line on the template. Snip along the curved edges, turn through to the right side and press well.

4. Take one body piece and one ear, and place the ear on top of the body piece, right sides together, so that the raw edge of the ear meets the front raw edge of the dart, aligning with the bottom of the dart. Easing the curve of the ear to match the curve of the dart edge, machine sew the ear into place (Fig. 2).

5. Now fold the body piece to position the two raw edges of the dart on top of each other, right sides together, so that the ear is between the two layers. Sew the dart into place, leaving a 5cm (2in) gap for turning in the centre of the ear section and easing your stitching to the folded edge as shown in Fig. 3.

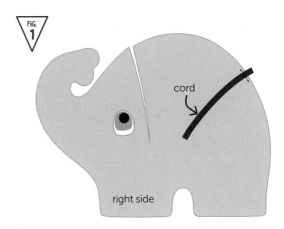

FiG. 1

cord

right side

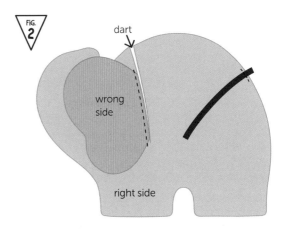

FiG. 2

dart

wrong side

right side

TiP: IF YOU ARE MAKING THIS TOY FOR A SMALL CHILD, OMIT THE BUTTON AND MAKE THE PUPIL OF THE ELEPHANT'S EYE BY WORKING A TRIPLE WRAP FRENCH KNOT (SEE STITCHING TECHNIQUES) USING ALL SIX STRANDS OF SIX-STRAND EMBROIDERY THREAD (FLOSS).

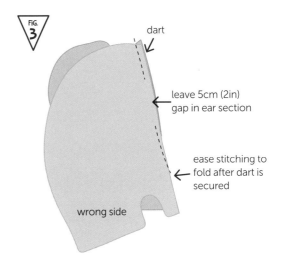

FiG. 3

dart

leave 5cm (2in) gap in ear section

ease stitching to fold after dart is secured

wrong side

6. Repeat steps 4 and 5 to join the remaining ear to the remaining body piece, but this time **do not** leave a turning gap.

7. Take one body piece and one inner leg piece, and place the inner leg piece on top of the body piece, right sides together. Referring to Fig. 4, machine sew the inner leg to the body ensuring that you start stitching right at the raw edge of the fabric and gradually turn into a 6mm (¼in) seam before tapering to the raw edge again at the other end. Repeat to join the remaining body and inner leg pieces.

8. Now sew the dart on the inner leg sections of the joined body/inner leg pieces. Fold each inner leg section in half, right sides together, so that the fold goes down the centre of the dart marking. Sew each dart into place in the inner leg only, following the marked dart line. Trim any excess fabric away from your darts.

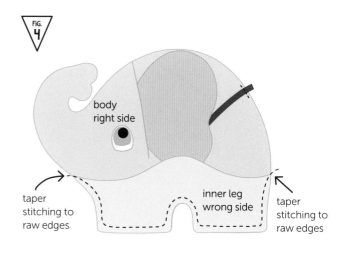

FIG. 4

body
right side

taper
stitching to
raw edges

inner leg
wrong side

taper
stitching to
raw edges

TiP: SEW THE INNER LEG DARTS INTO PLACE **AFTER** SEWING THE INNER LEGS TO THE BODY TO ENSURE THAT ALL OF THE LEG EDGES MATCH FLAT AND EVEN WHEN SEWING THEM TOGETHER.

9. Place the body pieces on top of each other, right sides facing (with the inner legs in between) and tack (baste) together: when you reach the inner leg section you need to ensure you are tacking (basting) the **top** edges of the inner legs together, right sides facing. It may be easier to do this by folding the legs up against either side of the body as shown in Fig. 5, but do check that the ears are clear of your tacking (basting) stitches.

10. Machine sew the body/inner leg pieces together, making sure that the ears are clear of your stitching.

11. Turn the elephant right side out through the turning gap (behind one of the ears); press the ears if required. Stuff your elephant firmly with toy filling (stuff the trunk first), then ladder stitch (see Stitching Techniques) the opening closed, adding a little more filling as you go to avoid a dimple.

12. To finish the elephant, tie a knot into the tail at the desired length and then trim off the excess.

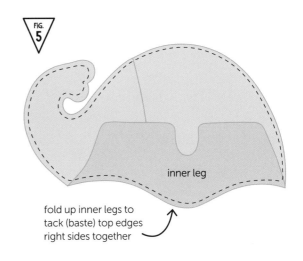

FiG. 5

inner leg

fold up inner legs to tack (baste) top edges right sides together

TiP: TO STUFF THE TRUNK, USE A STUFFING TOOL, SUCH AS THE BLUNT END OF A WOODEN SKEWER, TO MANOEUVRE SMALL PIECES OF FILLING TO THE VERY END OF THE TRUNK AND THEN STUFF FIRMLY FROM THERE.

KING OF THE FAIR

L ions are my favourite animal of all. If you are a big 'cat person', you can't help but be in awe of these majestic creatures. They look so cuddly yet command our respect. If, like me, you have always wanted one as a pet, why not make this fun fellow from bright cotton fabric with his sweet, smiley face framed by an eye-catching mane made from jumbo ric-rac.

YOU WILL NEED

Note: Buttons should be omitted if making this toy for a very small child. Use a 100% cotton patchwork fabric with a width of 106cm–114cm (42in–44in).

★ 21cm (8in) x the full fabric width of the main fabric (body, inner legs, head top)

★ 12.5cm x 50cm (5in x 20in) contrasting fabric (head bottom, ears, tail)

★ 7.5cm (3in) of matching cord for tail

★ 50cm (20in) of matching jumbo ric-rac for mane

★ 5cm x 6cm (2in x 2½in) brown 100% wool felt for nose

★ Brown six-strand embroidery thread (floss) in a shade to match wool felt

★ 5cm x 6cm (2in x 2½in) fusible web

★ Two small black buttons for eyes and black thread

★ Good-quality polyester thread

★ Good-quality polyester toy filling

FINISHED SIZE: 18cm (7in) tall x 22.5cm (8½in) long

CUTTiNG YOUR FABRiCS

Note: Trace the King of the Fair (red) templates (see Templates) onto tracing paper or template plastic, transferring all of the markings, and cut them out around the traced lines. When using these templates to trace the pattern pieces onto your fabric, do ensure that the marked grain line on the template matches the fabric grain line.

FROM YOUR MAiN FABRiC:

Fold the fabric in half with right sides together. Trace the body, inner leg and head top templates once onto the wrong side of the folded fabric transferring all markings. Cut out along the traced lines to give you two mirror-image pieces of each.

FROM YOUR CONTRASTiNG FABRiC:

Fold the fabric in half with right sides together and trace the head bottom template once onto the wrong side of the folded fabric. Cut out along the traced lines to give you two pieces. (You will use the remaining fabric for the tail and ears a little later, so set aside for now.)

PREPARiNG TO START

1. Trace the nose onto the paper side of the fusible web and rough cut out. Fuse this to the brown wool felt and cut out along the traced line.

2. Set your sewing machine to a small stitch length of approx 1.5 for stitching the toy and use a good-quality polyester thread for strong seams (if cotton thread is used, your seams could break during stuffing).

MAKiNG THE LioN

Note: A 6mm (¼in) seam allowance is included in all pattern pieces unless advised otherwise. Read through all instructions before beginning to avoid surprises.

1. Take the remaining piece of contrasting fabric and, still working with it folded (right sides together), trace the ear template twice and the tail template once onto the wrong side of the folded fabric, ensuring that you leave at least 1.3cm (½in) between each tracing. Machine sew along the traced lines of the ears and the tail, leaving the straight edges unstitched as indicated by the broken line on the template. Cut out the ears and the tail approx 3mm (⅛in) outside the sewn line, snip corners and turn right side out.

TiP: TO TURN OUT SMALL PIECES, SUCH AS THE LiON'S TAiL, iNSERT A PAiR OF TWEEZERS iNTO THE OPEN END OF THE PIECE TO BE TURNED, PINCH THE SEWN END AND PULL iT THROUGH.

2. Setting aside the ears for now, finish making the tail. Turn the raw edges in by approx 6mm (¼in) and finger press. Lightly stuff the tail with a little toy filling. Take the length of cord and tape one end to prevent it from fraying. Insert the taped end into the tail until the tape is enclosed within. Take small hand running stitches

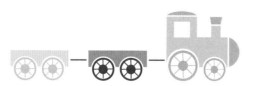

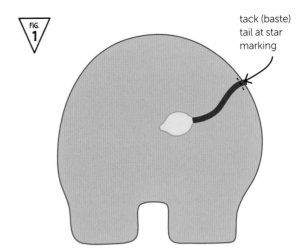

FiG. 1

tack (baste) tail at star marking

around the folded-in edge of the tail, then gather up the stitches so that the tail fits snugly over the cord. Finish by taking a few stitches through the cord itself to secure it. Trim the loose end of the cord to the desired tail length.

3. Position the completed tail onto the right side of one of the body pieces (see tail placement position indicated on the template), so that it is lying at an angle (see Fig. 1). Machine tack (baste) the tail into place close to the edge.

4. Take an inner leg piece and place on top of the body piece with tail attached, right sides together. Referring to Fig. 2, machine sew the inner leg to the body ensuring that you start stitching right at the raw edge of the fabric and gradually turn into a 6mm (¼in) seam before tapering to the raw edge again at the other end. Repeat to join the remaining body and inner leg pieces.

5. Now sew the dart on the inner leg sections of the joined body/inner leg pieces. Fold each inner leg section in half, right sides together, so that the fold goes down the centre of the dart marking. Sew each dart into place in the inner leg only, following the marked dart line. Trim any excess fabric away from your darts.

TiP: SEW THE INNER LEG DARTS INTO PLACE **AFTER** SEWING THE INNER LEGS TO THE BODY TO ENSURE THAT ALL OF THE LEG EDGES MATCH FLAT AND EVEN WHEN SEWING THEM TOGETHER.

FiG. 2

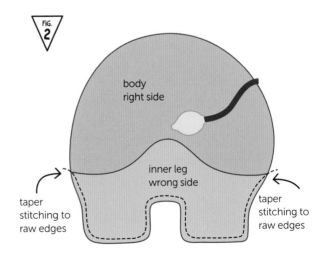

body right side

inner leg wrong side

taper stitching to raw edges

taper stitching to raw edges

6. Place the body pieces on top of each other, right sides facing (with the inner legs in between) and tack (baste) together. When you reach the inner leg section you need to ensure you are tacking (basting) the **top** edges of the inner legs together, right sides facing. It may be easier to do this by folding the legs up against either side of the body as shown in Fig. 3.

7. Machine sew the body together starting and ending at either end of the turning gap, indicated by a broken line on the template. Snip into the curves and angles of the inner leg before turning the lion's body right side out through the turning gap.

8. Stuff the lion's body very firmly with toy filling and ladder stitch the opening closed (see Stitching Techniques): as the stitching will be covered by the head, there is no need to worry about perfect stitching. Put the body aside for now.

9. Sew the dart into place on the bottom of the head pieces. Fold each piece in half, right sides together, so that the raw dart edges are on top of each other and machine sew using a 6mm (¼in) seam (see Fig. 4).

10. Take one head top and one head bottom piece and place together with right sides facing and straight edges aligning. Pin, then machine stitch together. Open out and press. Repeat to join the remaining head top and bottom pieces, but this time leave a 5cm (2in) turning gap in the centre of the seam.

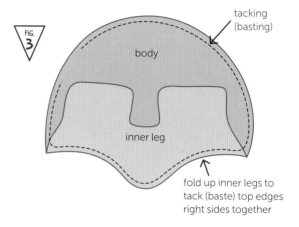

FiG. 3

tacking (basting)

body

inner leg

fold up inner legs to tack (baste) top edges right sides together

11. Position the ears onto the front of the head (without turning gap), right sides together, as shown in Fig. 5. Machine tack (baste) the ears in place.

12. Now arrange the jumbo ric-rac mane into place all the way around the edge of the front of the head, bearing in mind the 6mm (¼in) seam allowance. When you are happy with this, machine tack (baste) into place, close to the edge, carefully easing the ends of the ric-rac to the outside of the head to create a neat starting and ending point (see Fig. 6).

13. Place the head pieces together, right sides facing, ensuring that the lower face seams meet evenly at the sides; pin or tack (baste) in position. Machine sew all the way around the edge. Trim away the excess ric-rac, then turn the head right side out through the gap in the back of the head. Stuff the lion's head firmly with toy filling, then ladder stitch the opening closed.

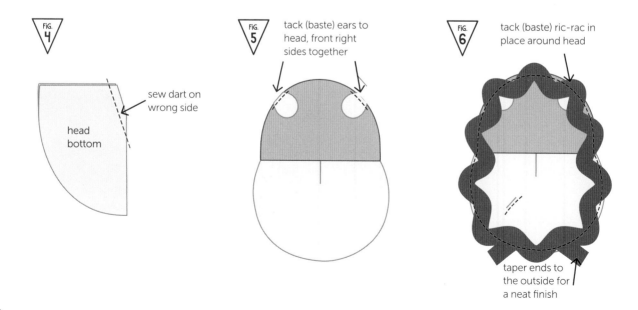

FiG. 4

sew dart on wrong side

head bottom

FiG. 5

tack (baste) ears to head, front right sides together

FiG. 6

tack (baste) ric-rac in place around head

taper ends to the outside for a neat finish

TIP: IF YOU ARE MAKING THIS TOY FOR A SMALL CHILD, SUBSTITUTE A SMALL PIECE OF BLACK WOOL FELT FOR THE BUTTONS, OR CREATE THE EYES WITH SATIN STITCH (SEE STITCHING TECHNIQUES).

14. Using black thread, sew the button eyes into place on the lion's face referring to the photograph for positioning. Take the brown felt nose, peel off the backing paper, and fuse it into place on the lion's head. Blanket stitch the nose to secure using two strands of brown embroidery thread (floss). Mark the mouth, whiskers and nose line onto the lion's face with a fabric marker, and backstitch over the lines using four strands of brown embroidery thread (floss), sinking your knot to finish (see Stitching Techniques).

15. Place the lion's head onto the front of the body so that it is lying on top of the turning gap, adjusting it until you are pleased with its position. Hand tack (baste) in place – I like to put the head on at a slight angle to give the toy a little extra personality.

16. Ladder stitch (see Stitching Techniques) the head onto the body using a double length of strong polyester thread. Essentially you will be stitching them together in an oval shape, where head meets body, surrounding (and so hiding) the turning gaps. Go around your stitching twice for added strength and keep your thread tension tight as you work to create a close, strong join.

TIP: WHEN YOU ARE HAPPY WITH WHERE THE HEAD IS SITTING, DO MAKE SURE THAT IT IS HIDING BOTH TURNING GAPS BEFORE TACKING (BASTING) IT INTO PLACE.

SEAL WITH A KISS

Seals are such clever, curious creatures and they put on quite a show at feeding time as they duck and dive for their favourite treats. With their sweet puppy-dog eyes and sleek gliding bodies, who could resist them? They are so easy to love and this delightful pair of seal pups would agree that nothing could possibly be better than a wet fishy kiss!

Note: Buttons should be omitted if making this toy for a very small child. Use a 100% cotton patchwork fabric with a width of 106cm–114cm (42in–44in).

(FOR ONE SEAL)

★ 32cm (12½in) x the full fabric width of the main fabric (body, head gusset, tail, flippers)

★ 12.5cm x 30cm (5in x 12in) contrasting fabric (tummy gusset)

★ Small scrap black 100% wool felt for nose

★ 20cm x 30cm (8in x 12in) lightweight fusible fleece

★ Small scrap of fusible web

★ Six-strand embroidery thread (floss): black and colour to match your main fabric for whiskers

★ Doll-maker's needle

★ Two small black buttons for eyes and black thread

★ Good-quality polyester thread

★ Good-quality polyester toy filling

FINISHED SIZE: 25cm (10in) tall x 32cm (12½in) long

CUTTING YOUR FABRICS

Note: Trace the Seal with a Kiss (pink) templates (see Templates) onto tracing paper or template plastic, transferring all of the markings, and cut them out around the traced lines. To make the full template join body 1 and body 2 templates along the dashed lines. When using these templates to trace the pattern pieces onto your fabric, do ensure that the marked grain line on the template matches the fabric grain line.

FROM YOUR MAIN FABRIC:

Fold the fabric in half with right sides together, then trace the body and tail templates once onto the wrong side of the folded fabric, transferring all markings. Cut out along the traced lines to give you two mirror-image pieces of each.

Opening out the remaining fabric to a single layer, trace the head gusset template once only and cut out along the traced line.

Also from single layer fabric, cut one piece measuring 20cm x 30cm (8in x 12in) for making the flippers.

FROM YOUR CONTRASTING FABRIC:

Trace the tummy gusset template once onto the fabric. Cut out along traced line.

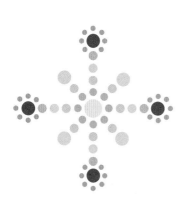

PREPARING TO START

1. Trace the nose onto the paper side of the fusible web and rough cut out. Fuse this to the black wool felt and cut out along the traced line.

2. Interface the 20cm x 30cm (8in x 12in) panel of main fabric with the matching piece of fusible fleece.

3. Set your sewing machine to a small stitch length of approx 1.5 for stitching the toy and use a good-quality polyester thread for strong seams (if cotton thread is used, your seams could break during stuffing).

MAKING THE SEAL

Note: A 6mm (¼in) seam allowance is included in all pattern pieces unless advised otherwise. Read through all instructions before beginning to avoid surprises.

1. Take one of the body pieces and the head gusset piece and place together, right sides facing, matching up the star markings so that one side of the head gusset aligns with the head part of the seal's body from nose to neck. Pin or tack (baste) in place then, referring to Fig. 1, machine sew the head gusset into position ensuring that you start stitching right at the raw edge of the fabric and gradually turn into a 6mm (¼in) seam before tapering to the raw edge again at the end of your stitching.

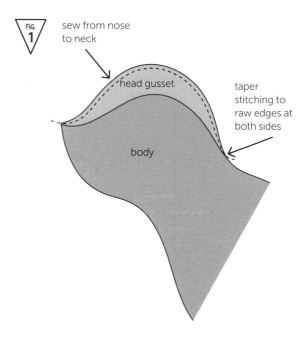

FIG. 1

sew from nose to neck

head gusset

taper stitching to raw edges at both sides

body

2. Take the remaining body piece and place this on top of the remaining raw edge of the head gusset piece, right sides together. Pin or tack (baste) the body piece along the head gusset, ensuring it is evenly matched up with the first body piece. When you reach the end of the head gusset, continue pinning or tacking (basting) the back of the main body pieces together until you reach the corner of the tail section. Check the fit, then machine sew together from nose to tail.

3. Place the two tail pieces right sides together and machine sew along the curved edges, leaving the straight edge open as indicated by the broken line on the template. Snip into the curved edges and inner angle, then turn right side out. Snip the bottom layer only along the snip line marked on the template.

4. Take the seal's body, open up at the tail end and lay this flat on your work surface, right side up. Now take the tail and open out from the slit to lay the full straight edge right sides together with the tail section of the body. Tack (baste) in place evenly and machine sew together (see Fig. 2).

5. Take the interfaced piece of main fabric and fold in half, right sides together. Trace the flipper template twice onto the wrong side of the folded panel, ensuring that there is at least 1.3cm (½in) between each tracing. Machine sew along the traced lines, leaving the straight edges open for turning as indicated by the broken line on the template. Cut out the flippers approx 3mm (⅛in) outside of the sewn line and snip along the curved edges. Turn right side out, press well and then topstitch close to the sewn edges. Mark the definition lines onto your flipper from the template and topstitch these lines into place stitching over the markings.

TIP: SNIPPING INTO CURVES AND ANGLES ON YOUR SEAM ALLOWANCES WILL HELP TO ENSURE A GOOD SHAPE IS ACHIEVED WHEN STUFFING. USING THE TIP OF YOUR SCISSORS, TAKE SMALL CUTS AND BE VERY CAREFUL NOT TO SNIP INTO YOUR STITCHES.

 FIG. 2

open out tail from slit and sew to opened up tail end of body

tail

body

6. Take one of the flippers and place it right sides together on top of one side of the seal's body, matching up the dot markings (see Fig. 3). Machine tack (baste) into place close to the edge. Repeat to join the second flipper to the other side of the body.

7. Take the tummy gusset piece and place one side of it along one side of the seal's body, matching up the square markings as your starting point. Ease and tack (baste) the pieces together making sure that you do not pull or stretch either piece; when you have finished there should be approx 5.5cm (2¼in) of the body piece remaining before the tail. Machine sew the tummy gusset into place, ensuring that you start stitching right at the raw edge of the fabric, gradually turn into a 6mm (¼in) seam and then taper to the raw edge again at the end of your stitching (see step 1). When sewing the section after the flipper, do make sure that you do not catch the free sides of the flipper in your stitching.

8. Repeat step 7 to join the remaining side of the tummy gusset to the remaining side of the body, but this time also tack (baste) the section from the nose to the tummy gusset and from the tummy gusset to the end of the tail slit. Machine sew all the way from the nose to the end of the tail slit, leaving the gap (after tummy gusset) open for turning as indicated by the broken line on the body template.

9. Snip the corner at the nose and then turn the seal's body right side out. Stuff firmly with toy filling, ensuring that you firmly stuff the head before continuing on to stuff the remainder of the body. Before stitching the opening closed, check that your seal stands properly with the flippers giving some support. Add more toy filling as necessary to achieve a good-standing seal. Once you are happy, ladder stitch (see Stitching Techniques) the opening closed.

10. Take the black felt nose, peel off the backing paper and position it over the nose point on the seal's face. Fuse the nose in place, then blanket stitch (see Stitching Techniques) to fix using two strands of black embroidery thread (floss). Backstitch (see Sewing Techniques) a smile approx 1.3cm (½in) below the nose.

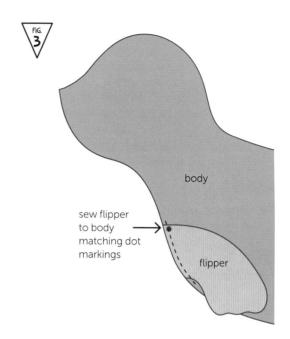

FIG. 3

body

sew flipper to body matching dot markings

flipper

TiP: IF YOU ARE MAKING THIS TOY FOR A SMALL CHILD, SUBSTITUTE A SMALL PIECE OF BLACK WOOL FELT FOR THE BUTTONS, OR CREATE THE EYES WITH SATIN STITCH.

11. Using black thread, sew the button eyes into place referring to the photograph for positioning.

12. Thread the doll-maker's needle with a long length of four strands of matching embroidery thread (floss) and tie a knot approx 2.5cm (1in) from the end. Decide where you want your whiskers to be, then take your needle through from one side of the nose to the other, pulling through until the knot catches. Now tie a knot right up against the fabric on this side and trim the thread approx 2.5cm (1in) from the knot. Repeat this process twice more.

TiP: IF THE SEAL'S NOSE IS NOT STUFFED FIRMLY ENOUGH, IT MAY BE NECESSARY TO GLUE TACK (BASTE) THE BLACK FELT NOSE IN PLACE PRIOR TO STITCHING (SEE STITCHING TECHNIQUES).

MONKEY MISCHIEF

On a day out at the zoo, I head straight for the monkeys – I could watch them for hours. They are so fascinating. Cheeky and mischievous, yet so incredibly loving, they have inspired me to create a pair of monkeys just for you. They are made from bright cotton fabric and pure wool felt for strength and washability. The she-monkey has a bow in her hair and he-monkey a dashing bow tie.

YOU WILL NEED

Note: Buttons should be omitted if making this toy for a very small child. Use a 100% cotton patchwork fabric with a width of 106cm–114cm (42in–44in).

(FOR ONE MONKEY)

★ 25cm (10in) x the full fabric width of the main fabric (body, head top, arms, legs, inner ears, nose back)

★ 18cm x 38cm (7in x 15in) contrasting fabric (shorts, bow/bow tie)

★ 25cm x 25cm (10in x 10in) 100% wool felt in colour to match main fabric (nose front, outer ears, chest patch, eye patch)

★ 10cm x 15cm (4in x 6in) fusible web

★ Black six-strand embroidery thread (floss)

★ Two small black buttons for eyes and black thread

★ Good-quality polyester thread

★ Good-quality polyester toy filling

FINISHED SIZE: 37cm (14½in) tall

CUTTiNG YOUR FABRiCS

Note: Trace the Monkey Mischief (blue) templates (see Templates) onto tracing paper or template plastic, transferring all of the markings, and cut them out around the traced lines. When using these templates to trace the pattern pieces onto your fabric, do ensure that the marked grain line on the template matches the fabric grain line.

FROM YOUR MAIN FABRiC:

Fold the fabric in half with right sides together, then trace the body and head top templates once onto the wrong side of the folded fabric, transferring all markings. Cut out along the traced lines to give you two mirror-image pieces of each.

Opening out the remaining fabric to a single layer, trace the nose back once only and cut out along the traced line.

Also, from single layer fabric, cut one piece measuring 7.5cm x 12.5cm (3in x 5in) for the inner ears.

Refold the remaining fabric and trace the leg and arm templates twice each on the wrong side of the fabric. **Do not** cut out.

FROM YOUR CONTRASTiNG FABRiC:

For the bow/bow tie, cut two strips measuring 5cm x 14cm (2in x 5½in) for the bow and one strip measuring 4.5cm x 7.5cm (1¾in x 3in) for the cincher (middle bit).

Trace the shorts template twice onto the remaining fabric and cut out along the traced lines.

FROM THE WOOL FELT:

Trace the nose front twice onto felt and cut out along the traced lines.

Cut one piece measuring 7.5cm x 12.5cm (3in x 5in) for the outer ears.

PREPARiNG TO START

1. Trace the eye patch and the chest patch shapes onto the paper side of the fusible web and rough cut out. Fuse to your remaining wool felt and cut the shapes out along the traced lines.

2. Set your sewing machine to a small stitch length of approx 1.5 for stitching the toy and use a good-quality polyester thread for strong seams (if cotton thread is used, your seams could break during stuffing).

MAKiNG THE MONKEY

Note: A 6mm (¼in) seam allowance is included in all pattern pieces unless advised otherwise. Read through all instructions before beginning to avoid surprises.

1. Take one head top and one body piece and fuse the eye patch and chest patch felt shapes onto these fabric pieces as marked on the templates. Using a matching thread colour, machine appliqué the eye patch and chest patch in place.

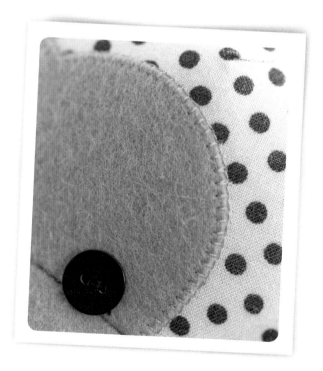

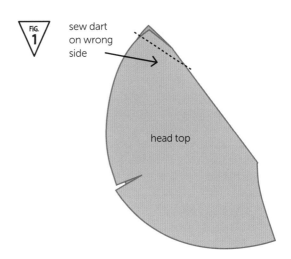

FIG. 1

sew dart on wrong side

head top

2. Sew the darts into place on the head top pieces. Fold each piece in half, right sides together, so that the raw dart edges are on top of each other and machine sew using a 6mm (¼in) seam (see Fig. 1).

3. Place the two felt nose front pieces on top of each other and pin, then sew along the curved edge only, tapering the stitching to and from the 6mm (¼in) seam allowance at either end (see Fig. 2). Turn through.

4. Take the joined nose front and the head top front (with eye patch) and place on top of each other, right sides together, ensuring that the head top front is centred within the raw edge of one side of the nose front. Machine sew together, easing the curve of the nose into the curve of the head top as you go. Once complete, the head front should look like Fig. 3 from the right side. Now join the nose back and the head top back in the same way.

5. Take the completed head front and place the bottom (raw) edge of the nose front on the neckline of the body front (with chest patch), right sides together. Centre the body within the nose and then machine sew together, easing the curve of the body into the curve of the nose as you go. Join the completed head back to the body back in the same way.

6. Place the joined head/body front and joined head/body back together, right sides facing, and pin or tack (baste) evenly all the way around the edge, ensuring that all seams meet neatly. Machine sew from one side to the other, leaving the bottom edge of the body open as indicated by the broken line on the template.

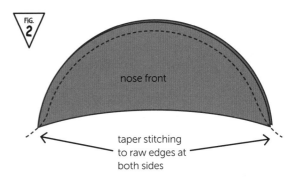

FIG. 2

nose front

taper stitching to raw edges at both sides

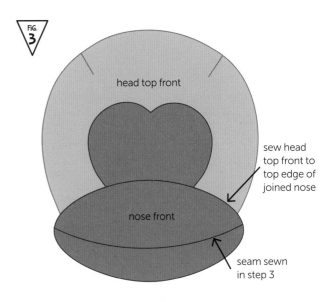

FIG. 3

head top front

nose front

sew head top front to top edge of joined nose

seam sewn in step 3

7. Remove the pins or tacking (basting) and turn the monkey right side out. Fold the bottom raw edge of the body in by approx 6mm (¼in) and press in place.

8. Take the main fabric piece with the arms and legs traced onto it, and stitch the arms and legs together by machine sewing along the traced lines, leaving the straight ends unstitched as indicated by the broken line on the templates. Cut out each limb approx 6mm (¼in) outside your sewn lines and then turn all pieces right side out.

9. Stuff the legs up to the indicated fill line (see template) and then machine sew across the fill line to secure. Tack (baste) the open ends together to hold them in place.

TiP: TO TURN A LIMB, OPEN AND REARRANGE THE FOOT/HAND END A LITTLE SO THAT YOU CAN PUSH A LONG, THIN STICK (CHOPSTICK OR WOODEN SKEWER) AGAINST THE SEWN END, THROUGH THE INSIDE OF THE LIMB AND OUT OF THE OPEN END.

10. Insert the legs between the folded edges at the base of the monkey's body, ensuring that the big toes are facing inwards and positioning each leg against the body seams to leave a gap in between (see Fig. 4). Tack (baste) in place, then machine topstitch through all layers, leaving the stuffing gap between the legs open.

11. Now stuff the monkey's head and body firmly with toy filling, then ladder stitch the neat folded-in opening between the legs closed (see Stitching Techniques).

12. Stuff the arms firmly, leaving the top 2.5cm (1in) only lightly stuffed to ensure that the jointing of the monkey's arm is floppy and relaxed for a realistic finished look. Turn the raw edges in by approx 6mm (¼in) and hand gather the folded edge. Working with

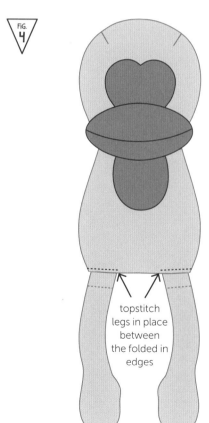

FIG. 4

topstitch legs in place between the folded in edges

32

two strands of strong polyester thread in your needle, take small running stitches all the way around the folded edges, then pull up the threads and secure the gathers with a knot. Ladder stitch (see Stitching Techniques) the arms in place at the sides of the body, referring to the photo of the finished monkey as a guide to positioning (the thumbs should be facing inwards). I recommend that you go around the ladder stitching two or three times.

TiP: IF YOU ARE MAKING THIS TOY FOR A SMALL CHILD, SUBSTITUTE A SMALL PIECE OF BLACK WOOL FELT FOR THE BUTTONS, OR CREATE THE EYES WITH SATIN STITCH (SEE STITCHING TECHNIQUES).

13. Using black thread, sew the button eyes into place on the monkey's face referring to the photograph for positioning. Use a pencil to mark on the monkey's mouth (see template) and nostrils, and stitch in place with four strands of black embroidery thread (floss) using backstitch for the mouth and French knots for the nostrils (see Stitching Techniques).

14. Now make the ears. Take the main fabric and wool felt squares each measuring 7.5cm x 12.5cm (3in x 5in) and place together, right sides facing. Trace the ear template onto the felt side, then machine sew along the traced lines, leaving the straight edges open. Cut out the ears approx 3mm–6mm (⅛in–¼in) outside the sewn lines. Snip around the curved edges before turning the ears right side out, then press the raw edges in neatly.

15. Using a strong polyester thread and referring to the photo of the finished monkey as a guide to positioning, ladder stitch the ears onto the monkey's face working first along the front edge, then along the back edge for added strength (see Stitching Techniques).

MAKING THE CLOTHES

Note: A 6mm (¼in) seam allowance is included in all pattern pieces unless advised otherwise.

1. Place the contrasting fabric shorts pieces together, right sides facing, and machine sew along the crotch lines (Fig. 5).

2. Open out the shorts and re-align them so that the front and back crotch seams (just sewn) are sitting on top of each other, right sides together. Now machine sew the shorts along the inner legs (as shown in Fig. 6).

3. Snip along all seams before turning the shorts right side out; press. To hem the legs of the shorts, fold under the edges by approx 6mm (¼in) and press; fold under again by another 6mm (¼in) and press once more; topstitch the double-fold hems into place. Now hem the waist: fold the edge under by 6mm (¼in), press, then topstitch in place.

4. Fit the shorts onto your monkey. If they are a little too loose, it just means that you have stuffed your monkey a little less than I did mine. Simply take a few ladder stitches in the shorts and the body side seams to secure the shorts in place (see Stitchig Techniques).

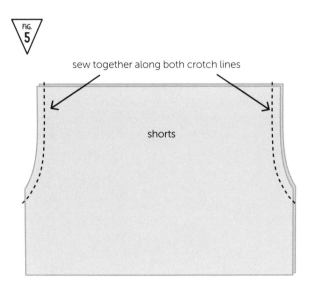

FIG. 5

sew together along both crotch lines

shorts

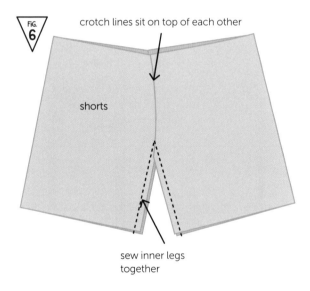

FIG. 6

crotch lines sit on top of each other

shorts

sew inner legs together

TiP: IF MONKEY'S SHORTS ARE STILL TOO LOOSE, YOU CAN HAND GATHER THE TOP EDGE A LITTLE BEFORE SECURING IN PLACE.

5. Now to make hair bow or bow tie. Take the two pieces of contrasting fabric measuring 5cm x 14cm (2in x 5½in), place together, with right sides facing, and machine sew each long edge. Turn to the right side and press well. Join the raw edges of the strip together to make a ring and hand tack (baste) to secure. Press the ring flat so that the join is at the centre bottom (Fig. 7). This is your bow piece.

6. Take the remaining piece of contrasting fabric for the cincher and fold this in half, right sides facing out, to create a folded strip measuring 7.5cm x 2.25cm (3in x ⅞in); press. Turn the raw edges in to the fold and press again. Topstitch along the long edges of the strip. Use the completed cincher strip to wrap around and gather the centre of your bow piece, covering the join at the back of your bow in the process. Sew the ends of the cincher strip together with small hand stitches to the tightness desired and trim away any excess.

7. Attach the bow onto your monkey's head or neck by ladder stitching along the top and bottom of the cincher (see Sewing Tehniques), to hide the seam against the toy.

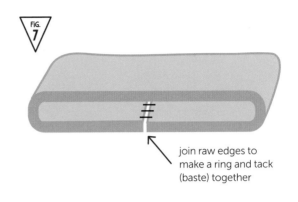

FIG. 7

join raw edges to make a ring and tack (baste) together

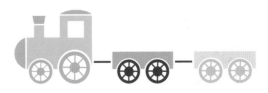

35

STITCHING TECHNIQUES

BACKSTITCH

Backstitch creates a continuous line of stitching, so it is ideal for creating facial features on your toys.

RUNNING STITCH

This simple stitch is used for gathering, as on the top edge of the lion's tail, and also for hand tacking (basting) pieces together.

BLANKET STITCH

This edging stitch is used to secure appliquéd fabric pieces such as the lion's nose.

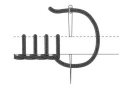

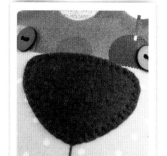

FRENCH KNOT

The double wrap French knot creates a prominent raised dot which is ideal for small facial features such as monkey's nostrils or pupils.

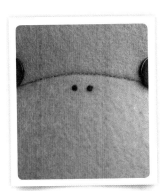

SATIN STITCH

This can be used as a substitute for button eyes when making toys for very young children. First backstitch around the outside edge of a circle shape and then work stitches from one side to the other, keeping them close and even.

SINKING A KNOT

When button jointing legs, or completing any stitching on a toy that is already stuffed, you will want to avoid any knots being visible where you start and end your stitching, so for a neat finish you will need to sink your knot into the toy. When you have completed the required sewing, tie a knot in the thread close to where it exits the toy. Take one last stitch into the toy, taking your needle through to an inconspicuous area approx 2.5cm–5cm (1in–2in) away. Pull the thread through and it will snag when the knot reaches the fabric where you started your stitch. Hold the thread firmly and tug it quickly so that the knot pops into the toy. Snip the thread end away right where it exits the fabric so that it too sinks into the toy.

LADDER STITCH

ATTACHING PARTS

One of the uses for ladder stitch is to attach parts to soft toys. This method is usually used so that the attachment will either sit flat against or protrude from the stuffed toy. Follow the ladder stitch diagram for closing gaps, but make one stitch in the edge of the attachment, then make the next stitch in the body of the toy. The ladder stitches need to be sewn into the body following the shape of the attachment so that the attached part retains its shape.

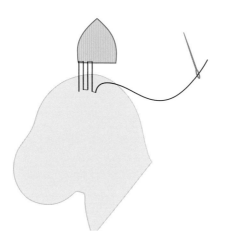

CLOSING GAPS

Use ladder stitch to sew turning gaps closed in a neat, strong and nearly invisible way.

TEMPLATES

PONY RIDES

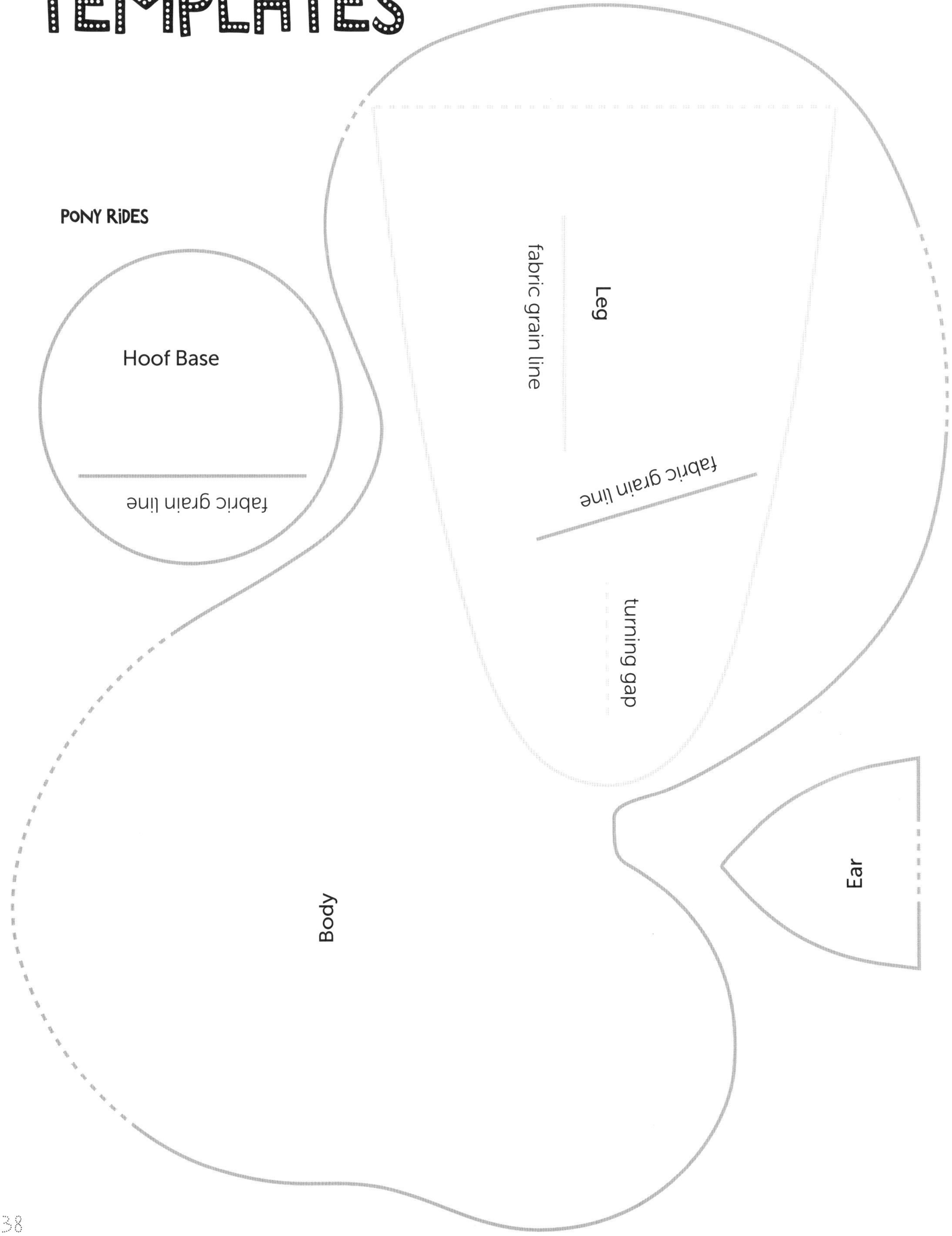

Hoof Base

fabric grain line

Leg

fabric grain line

fabric grain line

turning gap

Body

Ear

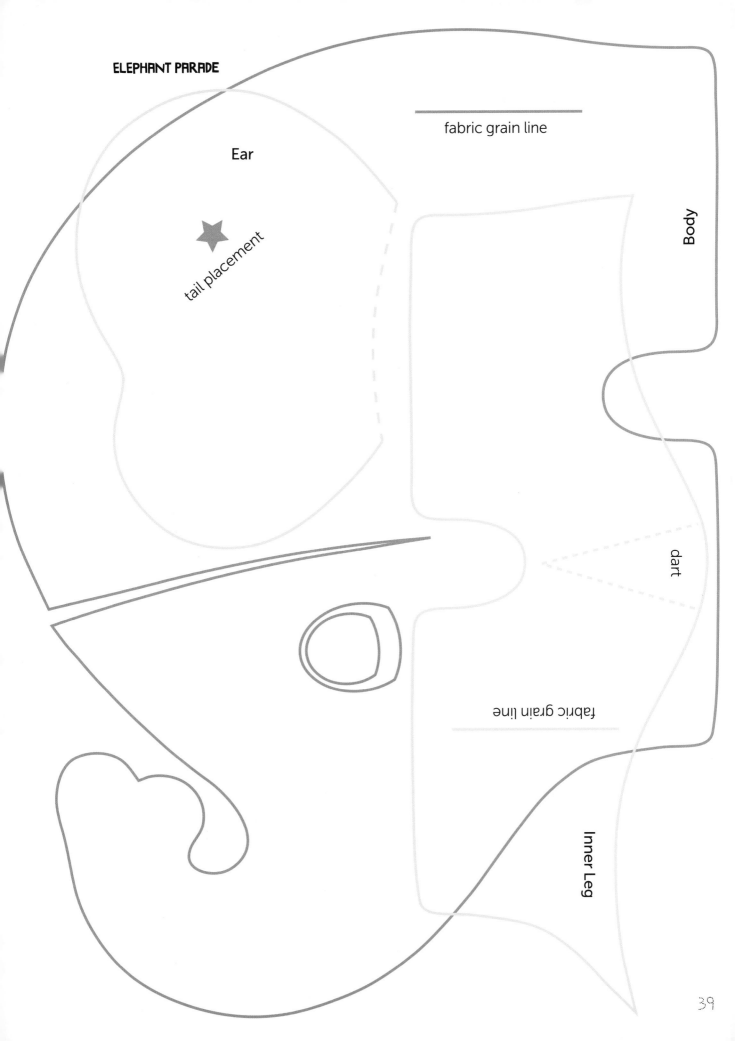

Ear

fabric grain line

Body

tail placement

dart

fabric grain line

Inner Leg

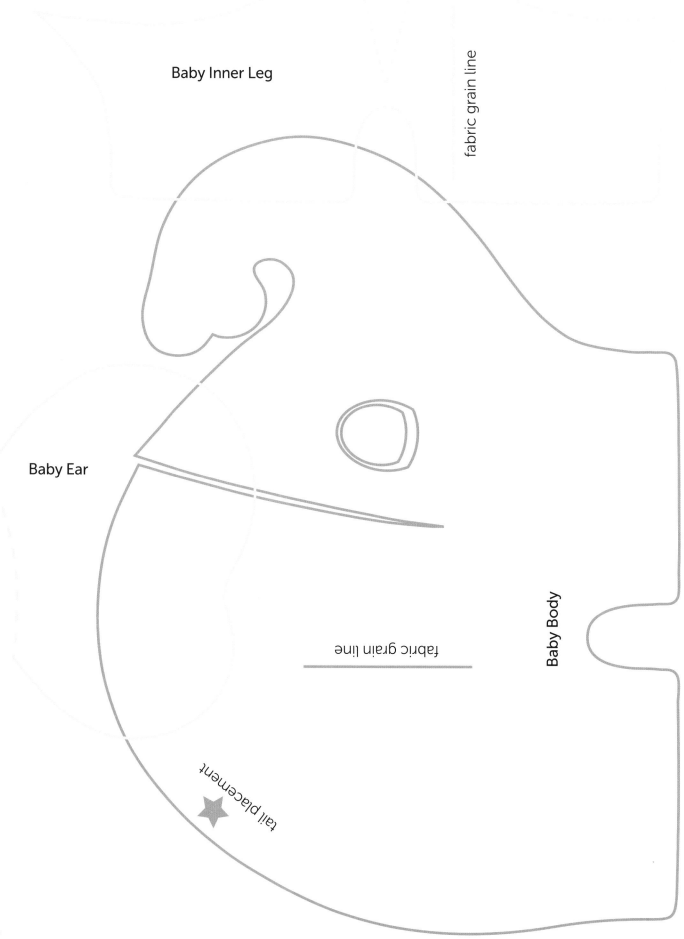

dart

Baby Inner Leg

fabric grain line

Baby Ear

Baby Body

fabric grain line

tail placement

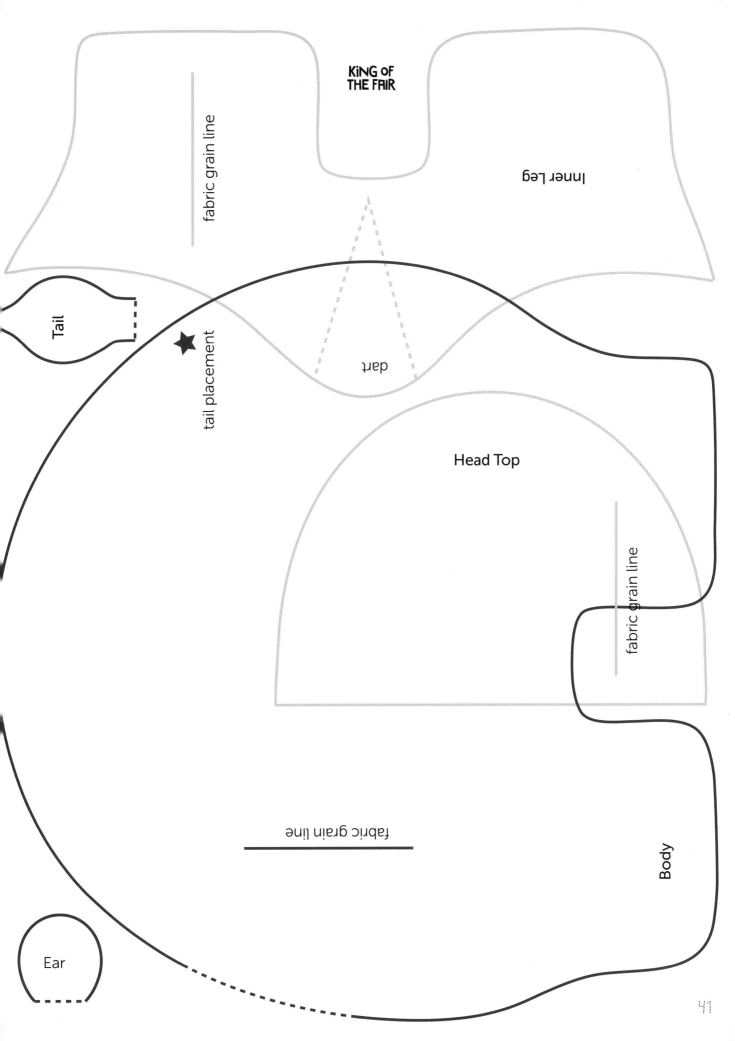

KING OF
THE FAIR

fabric grain line

Inner Leg

Tail

★ tail placement

dart

Head Top

fabric grain line

fabric grain line

Body

Ear

41

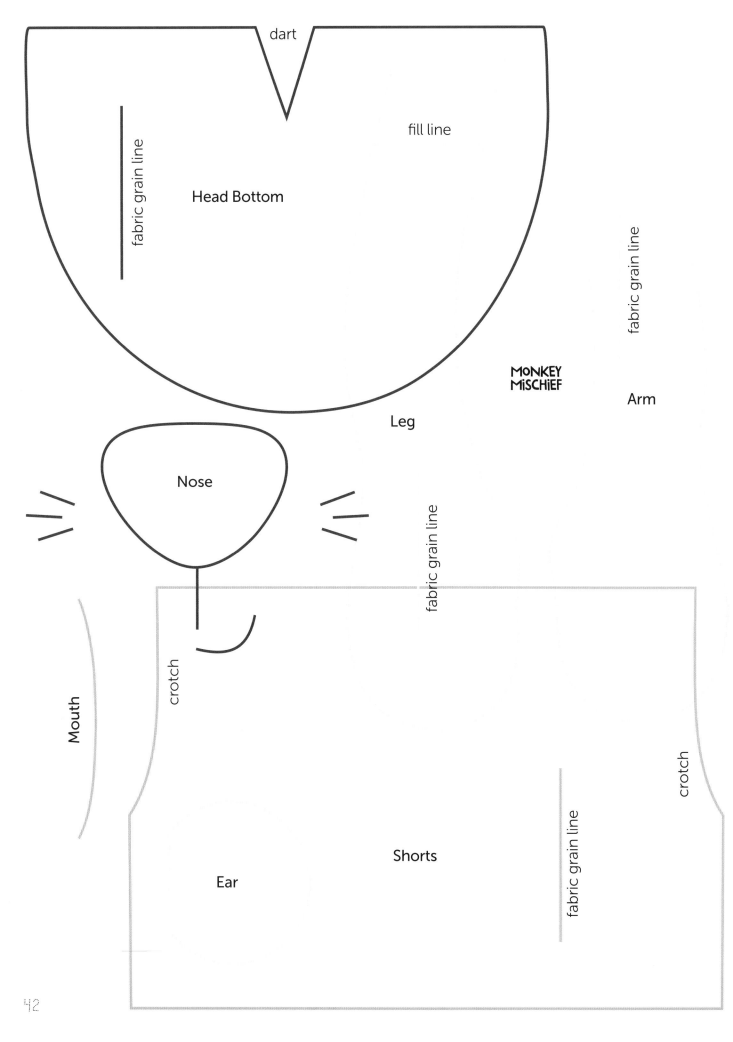

dart

fill line

fabric grain line

Head Bottom

fabric grain line

MONKEY
MiSCHiEF

Arm

Leg

Nose

fabric grain line

crotch

Mouth

crotch

Shorts

Ear

fabric grain line

Nose Back

fabric grain line

Chest Patch

Body

fabric grain line

Head Top

fabric grain line

Eye Patch

Nose Front

43

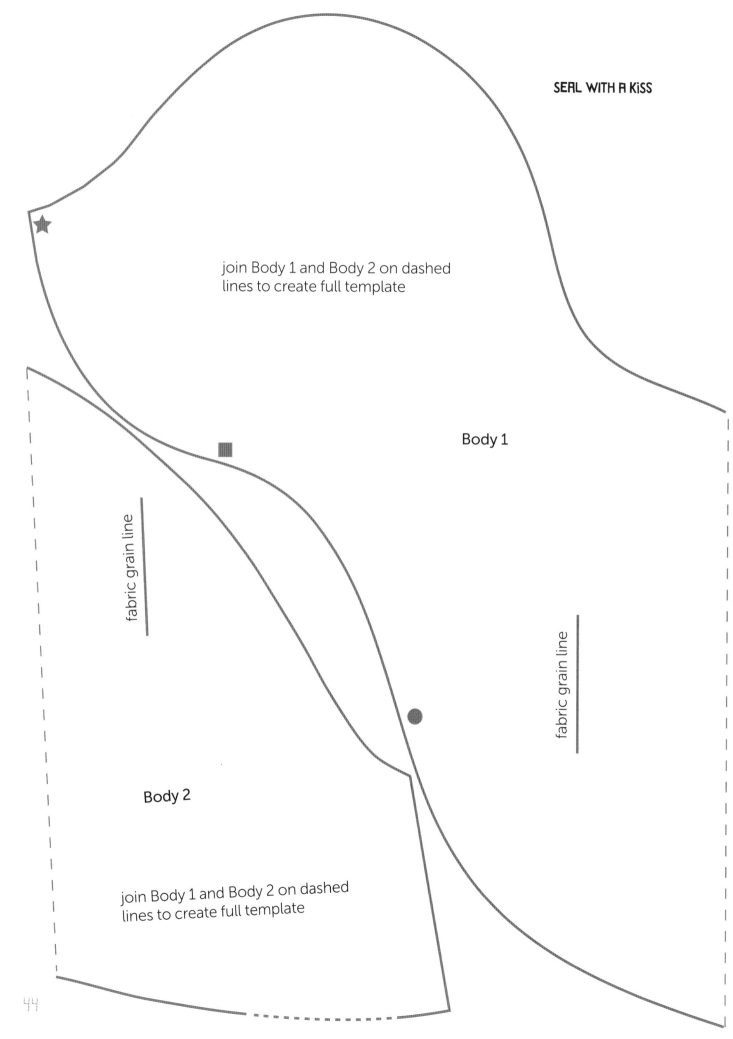

SEAL WITH A KiSS

join Body 1 and Body 2 on dashed
lines to create full template

Body 1

fabric grain line

fabric grain line

Body 2

join Body 1 and Body 2 on dashed
lines to create full template

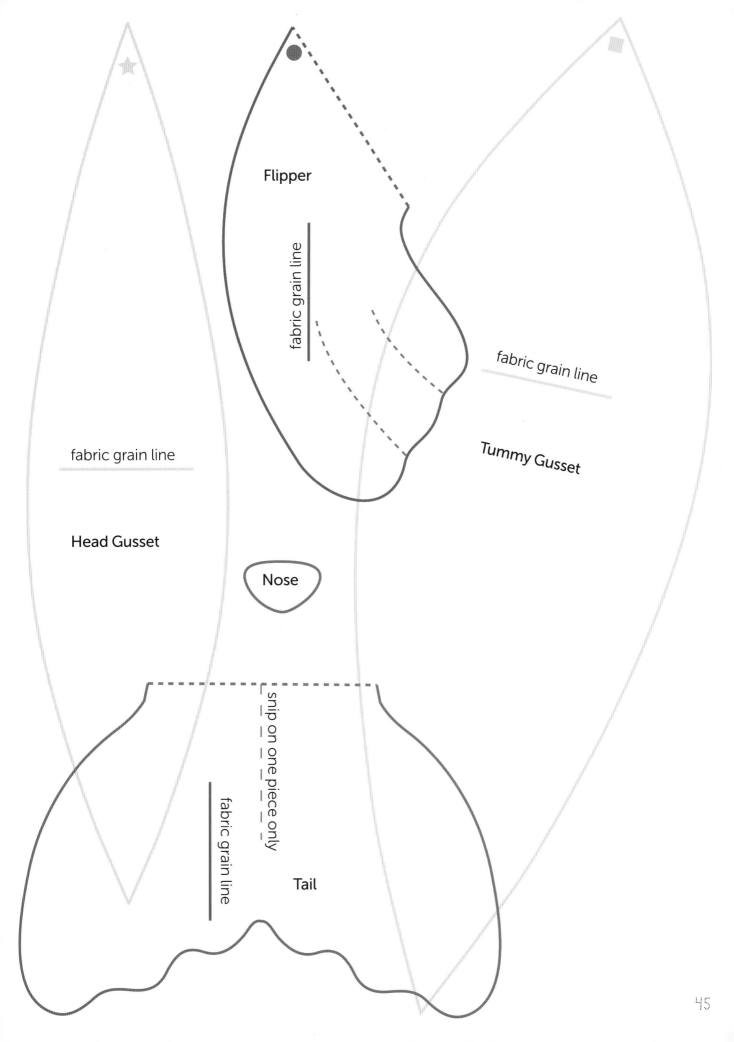

Flipper

fabric grain line

fabric grain line

Tummy Gusset

fabric grain line

Head Gusset

Nose

snip on one piece only

fabric grain line

Tail

45

ABOUT THE AUTHOR

Melanie McNeice is an Aussie pattern designer based in the leafy outskirts of Melbourne, Australia. Melly's adventures in sewing began just ten years ago after she found herself a stay-at-home mum with the desire to still be productive. Melly's passion for sewing grew quickly after her sister encouraged her to give it a try, and only 12 months after beginning to sew, she tried her hand at design under the pattern label Melly & me.

Melly's goals in design are to create a range of contemporary sewing patterns that include bright and quirky toys, wearable purses, as well as fun and modern quilts. Melanie aims to design items that are original and fun, achievable in a day, as well as being completely useable in everyday life! Melly & me has grown to appeal to a worldwide audience, and Melly has designed in excess of 100 patterns, published four books, *Kaleidoscope*, *Sewn Toy Tales*, *Snug as a Bug* and *Sew Cute to Carry*, and teaches across Australia. In 2010 Melly also began her journey in fabric design and has released five fabric collections since then.

Melly takes inspiration from her two young children, childhood memories, the beauty of nature, and her love of fun and colour. Visit Melly's website to see more of her fun designs at www.mellyandme.com.

THANKS!

This book is dedicated to all of the fabulous softie sewers out there who enjoy creating my designs and making them their own, as well as to all the warm arms that are cuddling a Melly & me toy!

Thank you to my three super test sewers – Christina MacNeil, Joanna Austin and Kelsie Clark, who tested these patterns out for me in the speediest of timeframes – you girls are the best!!!

Thank you to all at David & Charles for working with me on another fun project.

And always, a big thank you to my most amazing family – Scott, Zak and Kiki you are my rock, my loves, my everything!

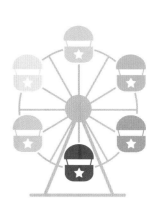

SUPPLIERS

Australia

Melly & Me
www.mellyandme.com
mellyandme@bigpond.com

Under the Mulberry Tree
www.underthemulberrytree.com

The Oz Material Girls
www.theozmaterialgirls.com

Fabric Patch
www.fabricpatch.com.au

Patchwork with Gail B
www.patchworkwithgailb.com

Creative Abundance
www.creativeabundance.com.au

USA

Pink Chalk Fabrics
www.pinkchalkfabrics.com

Pine Needles
www.pineneedlesonline.com

Heartsong Quilts
www.heartsongquilts.com

UK

Hulu Crafts
www.hulacrafts.co.uk

Prints to Polka Dots
www.printstopolkadots.co.uk

Stitch Craft Create
www.stitchcraftcreate.co.uk

The Fat Quarters
www.thefatquarters.co.uk

INDEX

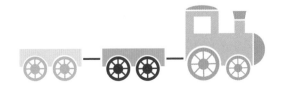

A DAVID & CHARLES BOOK
© F&W Media International, Ltd 2014

David & Charles is an imprint of F&W Media International, Ltd
Brunel House, Forde Close, Newton Abbot, TQ12 4PU, UK

F&W Media International, Ltd is a subsidiary of F+W Media, Inc
10151 Carver Road, Suite #200, Blue Ash, OH 45242, USA

Text and Designs © Melanie McNeice 2014
Layout and Photography © F&W Media International, Ltd 2014

First published in the UK and USA in 2014

A catalogue record for this book is available from the British Library.

ISBN-13: 978-1-4463-0519-5
ISBN-10: 1-4463-0519-8

Printed in China by RR Donnelley for:
F&W Media International, Ltd
Brunel House, Forde Close, Newton Abbot, TQ12 4PU, UK

10 9 8 7 6 5 4 3 2 1

Acquisitions Editor: Sarah Callard
Editor: Matthew Hutchings
Project Editor: Cheryl Brown
Art Editor: Anna Fazakerley
Photographer: Jack Kirby
Senior Production Controller: Kelly Smith

F+W Media publishes high quality books on a wide range of subjects.
For more great book ideas visit: www.stitchcraftcreate.co.uk